A gift for

From

Tiny Tidings of Joy

for You

Illustrations by Amy Rosenberg

COUNTRYMAN

Babbling Brook
Little Works of Heart

Published by J. Countryman,
a division of Thomas Nelson, Inc.,
Nashville, Tennessee 37214

Project Editor: Terri Gibbs

Designed by Left Coast Design Inc.,
Portland, Oregon

ISBN: 08499-9667-8

www.jcountryman.com

Printed in USA

A tiny tiding
sent to say:
"May your heart be
filled with laughter
each and every day!"

One can never spend
too much time
with a friend.

Children laughing
in the snow,
stockings hanging
in a row,
when merry days
of cheer begin,
Christmas fills our
hearts again.

When you
can't resist
the impulse to give . . .

just do it
with all
your heart!

If I could give you any gift at all I'd choose to give you:

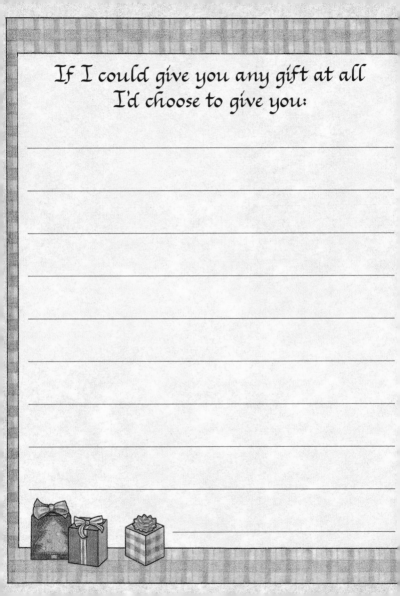

Every gift that's given

is a little bit of heaven.

Hearts go home
at Christmas...

home to those we love.

Celebrate the season
with a song!

Love came down
so meek and mild,
it was God's gift—
a newborn child.

Happy Holidays

A smile
can warm
the coldest
day.

Blessed be the LORD your God

who has delighted in you. 1 Kings 10:9

These are some of the things
I find delightful about you:

_____

_____

_____

_____

_____

_____

_____

_____

Let heaven's angels sing!!

Laughter
and joy,
like stars
in the night,
fill the world
with a
shining light.

A little Christmas prayer for you:

_____

_____

_____

_____

_____

_____

_____

_____

_____

Snow is falling here and there,
children laugh without a care . . .

Christmas tidings fill the air,
spreading great joy everywhere!

May
each day
of the season
give you
reason
to rejoice!

Life can be snow much fun!!

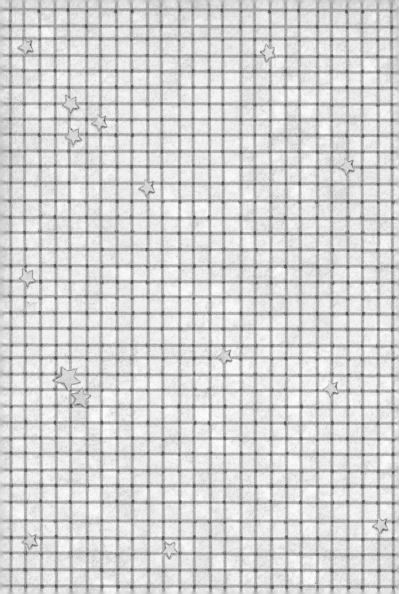